THE HOURS OF
JEANNE
D'ÉVREUX

THE HOURS OF

JEANNE D'ÉVREUX

QUEEN OF FRANCE

AT THE CLOISTERS

THE METROPOLITAN MUSEUM OF ART

MCMLVII

Published by The Metropolitan Museum of Art, New York

All rights reserved, 1957

Pages of reproductions engraved and printed in Paris
by Draeger Frères; text printed in New York
by Clarke and Way, Inc.; cover paper
printed by the Meriden Gravure Co.;
binding by Russell Rutter Co.

LIBRARY OF CONGRESS CATALOG CARD NUMBER: 57–9363

INTRODUCTION

THE MEDIEVAL BOOK OF HOURS was a private service and prayer book. It was so called because the prayers it contained were arranged according to the eight canonical hours of the day when they were recited by the individual. This type of book first appeared in the second half of the thirteenth century and increased in popularity until it became, during the fourteenth century, the most common form of private prayer book.

By their very nature such prayer books were highly personal and often exacted the skillful and patient work of the greatest artists of the day. For the excellence of its drawings and the originality and vitality of its decoration, the Book of Hours of Jeanne d'Évreux is acknowledged an outstanding example, a masterpiece of the developed Gothic courtly art of France. This extraordinary manuscript came to the New York art market in 1953

from the collection of Baron Maurice de Roth-
schild and was acquired for The Cloisters the following year.

Of the 209 folios comprising the original Book
of Hours, forty-eight characteristic pages, includ-
ing all the full-page pictures, are here illustrated.
The single example shown in actual size duplicates
the minuteness and exquisite delicacy of the paintings, decorations, and writing of the original. The
other pages are reproduced at one and a half times
their actual size, providing, as it were, an almost
necessary magnifying glass for the reader.

Aside from the principal illuminations, which
speak so eloquently for themselves, the droll and
grotesque figures decorating the margins and line
endings of these pages, also drawn with great skill,
may well excite our wonder. To modern eyes
these drolleries and grotesques must at times seem
both irrelevant and irreverent in a book of prayer.
The motives were drawn from many sources as-
sociated with the religious life of the Middle Ages.
What appears profane to us may have been in-
tended to suggest a moral lesson learned from the

antics of animals or extolled in the popular litera-
ture or morality plays of the time. The medieval
man had time for play and fun. If there were to be
outlets for humor, a private prayer book was a
place for the whimsy of the imaginative artist.
Apart from any meaning these decorative addi-
tions may suggest, they constitute a considerable
part of the charm of Jeanne d'Évreux's Book of
Hours.

While there is no positive proof establishing
the identification of The Cloisters book, neverthe-
less, from the date of its first major publication in
1910 by Léopold Delisle, numerous points of
correspondence with documents and fact have led
scholars to agree almost without exception that it
is the Book of Hours illustrated by Jean Pucelle
for Jeanne d'Évreux as a gift from her husband,
Charles IV of France. In the queen's will the
description, "a rather tiny little book of prayers . . .
which Pucelle illuminated," accords with our
manuscript, which measures 3⅝ by 2⅜ inches. It
could very well have been illuminated in 1325 at
the time of her marriage to Charles IV. In any

case, it must have been finished before Charles's death in 1328. The work mentioned in Jeanne's will passed in 1370 to King Charles V and then to his brother, the famous bibliophile, John of France, Duke of Berry. Three successive inventories of the Duke's treasures from 1401 to 1416 refer to the book as "a small Book of Hours of Our Lady, called the Hours of Pucelle."

All the documents stress the small size of the Hours of Jeanne d'Évreux. They further specify that it was "illuminated in black and white," a characterization which agrees with the predominance of grisaille, or black-and-white, illustrations in The Cloisters manuscript. The Duke of Berry's inventory described the little book as *à l'usaige des Prescheurs* (for the use of the Dominican preaching friars). The "captions" of the two main divisions of the text of this prayer book state in fact that the prayers are arranged according to the use of the *predicatores* (preachers).

In identifying The Cloisters Book of Hours with that of Jeanne d'Évreux one cannot overlook the fact that a youthful queen is portrayed below the Annunciation and in the anteroom to the left of the chapel in the scene depicting a miracle of Saint Louis, where a crowned figure is shown in prayer. These opening illustrations to the textual divisions often depict the person for whom the book was originally destined.

Most important for the attribution to Jean Pucelle are the stylistic similarities between The Cloisters Hours and the few documented works by the master. Little is known about his life. The earliest reference to Pucelle appears in a record of about 1320 which shows that he was already a practicing artist in Paris. In the absence of real evidence we can only suppose that he died before the middle of the century. Two manuscripts of the 1320s in the Bibliothèque Nationale mention his name and provide the basis of our knowledge of his art. A Bible known by the name of the scribe who signed it, Robert de Billyng, contains a dated colophon of 1326 naming Jehan Pucelle, Anciau de Sens, and Jacquet Maci as the illuminators. The Belleville Breviary, also in the Bibliothèque Nationale and supposedly written not later than 1326,

[9]

names the same masters, Jehan Pucelle, Anciau de Sens, and Jacquet Maci, and yet another, J. Chevrier, as participants in the production. The names are not given in the usual colophon but are preserved in workshop memoranda of payments to the artists. Since these indicate that it was Jehan Pucelle who made the payments to the others, they establish his position as the leading master in the collaboration.

A comparison of the narginal figures and scenes in the Hours of Jeanne d'Évreux with those in the Belleville Breviary reveals frequent and close relationships in invention and in modeling. Unlike the Breviary and the Paris Bible of Billyng, however, in which the assistants participated, The Cloisters manuscript may be considered a highly individual and personal achievement of Jean Pucelle himself. One of the most striking features of the Hours of Jeanne d'Évreux is the homogeneous excellence of the scenes and decoration, which is sustained throughout. To his Paris contemporaries Pucelle's illuminations must have seemed remarkable. Some of the subjects and many compositional and formalized concepts appear for the first time in Northern painting. The Annunciation is set in an interior drawn with convincing and coherent perspective. As a correlative of this new rendering of depth the figures are modeled in fluid and continuous gradations which, coupled with the use of monochrome, lends them a suggestion of palpable volume as they occupy the little "stage." Pucelle's interest in dramatic gestures and action, and in emotional concentration of figure groupings (seen in the Entombment and the Crucifixion), also introduces new standards for Northern Gothic art. The success of these artistic ideas is reflected in the numerous copies and adaptations of Pucelle's paintings found in manuscripts during the rest of the fourteenth century, and even later. The Italian masters Duccio and Giotto anticipated Pucelle in these innovations and they were, in fact, his sources. But, as Professor Erwin Panofsky has pointed out in his *Early Netherlandish Painting*, the real genius of Pucelle lay in the manner in which he used as his own the most advanced artistic language of Italy.

It was Pucelle who made available to the North the first completely intelligible French translation of Italian developments. For the rest of the history of Northern illumination artists continued to exploit the perspective illusion of pictorial depth on the page surface until the single miniature became the equivalent of a panel painting and the picture simulated a view of the world framed by an open window. On the broad horizons of the European *trecento* the significance of The Cloisters Pucelle manuscript for the development of Northern painting is comparable to that of Duccio's Maestà or Giotto's Arena Chapel frescoes for Italian painting.

Notwithstanding his Italianate interests Pucelle remained a Northerner. This is best seen in the treatment of the marginal illustrations. The use of drolleries and border scenes not only continues a deep-rooted tradition of the Netherlands, northern France, and England, but also carries it to new heights. Whereas such illustrations had been more or less independent of the main scenes on the page, with Pucelle they began to function more positively in relation to the scene. In the Belleville

Breviary they are an essential component of a highly organized pictorial program, a veritable counterpoint to the main sequence of subjects. This integration is in an early phase in The Cloisters Hours. Already some marginal figures become caryatids, supporting the framed illustration. Others are used to amplify the principal scene, as in the miniature of the Resurrection. While the meaning of the figures and scenes in the lower margins is not always intelligible to us, we recognize many that serve as incidental commentary and exegesis on the main subject, as in the Flight into Egypt with the falling pagan idols below, or as in the Massacre of the Innocents in the border below the Adoration of the Magi. Among the scenes from the life of Saint Louis the margins depict beggars and cripples, or medical subjects, clear allusions to the works of charity and healing of Saint Louis, King of France.

Unlike official church service books, such as the breviary, the Book of Hours could and did vary considerably in length, content, and arrangement of the offices. In essence its contents include a calendar as guide to feasts and to saints' days, excerpted readings from the Gospels, the Office of the Virgin, the Office of the Dead, the Penitential Psalms, and the Litany of the Saints. The canonical hours indicated for prayer are Matins, the first hour for prayers, which were recited originally at midnight, followed by Lauds at sunrise, Prime at six a.m., Terce at nine a.m., Sext at noon, None at three p.m., Vespers at sunset, and Compline, closing the day at nine p.m.

The Cloisters manuscript opens with the Calendar, followed by the Hours of the Virgin, the Hours of Saint Louis, the Seven Penitential Psalms, and the Litanies. Prefixed to each of the canonical hours in the Office of the Virgin is a pair of scenes, one from the life of the Virgin, the other from the Passion of Christ. As frontispiece to the Penitential Psalms the Majesty of Christ is depicted. The Hours of Saint Louis are accompanied by scenes from his life, one to each of the hours of the liturgical day.

The presence of the Hours of Saint Louis in this manuscript is particularly interesting as an indication of the enthusiastic cult of this king among ladies of the highest court circles. The office is included in the Hours of Jeanne de Navarre, daughter of Louis X, datable between 1336 and 1349. It was the widow of Saint Louis who founded the convent of the Cordelières de Lourcine, and their daughter Blanche who, early in the fourteenth century, commissioned for the cloister of the convent a series of paintings illustrating the life of Saint Louis. Though the frescoes are known today only through seventeenth-century descriptions and some drawings, Émile Mâle showed that there was a significantly close iconographic connection between the lost cycle and the scenes in the Hours of Jeanne d'Évreux. Still another group of paintings of the same period, treating the same theme and possibly also deriving from the lost frescoes, were to be seen in the lower chapel of the Sainte-Chapelle as late as the seventeenth century. It may well be that the frescoes of Lourcine, which antedated our manuscript, inspired Jean Pucelle. The scenes in the manuscript which are known to have appeared in the frescoes tend to have more traditional ornamental backgrounds in preference to the new architectural perspectives, and also a larger figure scale than those seen in the Life of the Virgin series.

Delisle's publication of the Hours of Jeanne d'Évreux, issued almost two generations ago, is practically unavailable to modern readers. The present Metropolitan Museum of Art version published for The Cloisters will serve to introduce a new public to this gem among Gothic illuminations. From such a leaf as the Annunciation it is apparent that the manuscript was originally slightly larger. It was cropped, parts of the border decoration and the tops of certain miniatures being cut off, probably at the time when its 27 gatherings of 209 folios were rebound for its seventeenth-century owners, Louis Jules du Châtelet and his wife, Christine de Gleseneuve, whose arms adorn the present red morocco binding. Whenever it was necessary to square the pages of the following reproductions, the missing parts were photographed on a background matching the color and texture of the original vellum. The reproductions are the faithful work of Draeger Frères in Paris.

I wish particularly to thank Dr. Harry Bober, who did the major work in helping me prepare the foregoing text, and my colleagues at The Cloisters and in the Publications Department who worked with me on the preparation of this book. The Cloisters Fund, generously provided by Mr. John D. Rockefeller, Jr., made possible the purchase and publication of the manuscript.

James J. Rorimer, DIRECTOR
THE METROPOLITAN MUSEUM OF ART

LIST OF
REPRODUCTIONS

*The pages of the manuscript were not originally num-
bered and reference numbers have been omitted from the
pages of reproduction. The odd numbers below indicate
the right, or recto, pages, even numbers the left, or verso,
pages. To facilitate identification, color reproductions are
indicated in the following titles by (c), monochrome reproductions by (m); further, confronting illustrations are
separated by a starred space from preceding and following
pairs of illustrations.*

[4] *Text Page of Matins of the Hours of the Virgin*.
(m) The drolleries include a modish woman and
a man shouldering a yoke with two buckets, like
those used for bath water.   FOL. 19V

[5] *Text Page of Matins*. (m) The line endings
show two figures seated on beasts. The bearded
man, above, is being bitten as he fights with arrow
and shield. Below, the hooded figure holds a beg-
ging bowl.   FOL. 20

★

[6] *Christ before Pilate*. (c) The monster caryatid
at the right is blowing a reed pipe which ends in
a cow horn.   FOL. 34V

[7] *The Visitation*. (c) The half figure of a soldier
within the initial, stalking the rabbit in the right
margin, is a parody of valor.   FOL. 35

★

[8] *The Flagellation*. (m) One of the caryatids in
the border holds a flail.   FOL. 53V

[9] *The Nativity*. (m) The figures in the lower
margin include acrobats, a monster-king playing
on a large jawbone while a dog dances, and a youth
putting a rock.   FOL. 54

[10] *Christ Carrying the Cross.* (c) One of the caryatids carries a hammer. FOL. 61V

[11] *The Annunciation to the Shepherds.* (c) The marginal illustrations continue and elaborate the scene. FOL. 62

★

[12] *Text Page of Terce of the Hours of the Virgin.* (m) The lines end in a dog, a rabbit, and monsters. Beneath the initial a doctor examines a flask with the aid of his medical book. FOL. 65V

[13] *Text Page of Terce.* (m) Three monsters end the lines and extend into the margin. FOL. 66

★

[14] *The Crucifixion.* (c) The miniature follows the composition of Duccio's Maestà in Siena, which was finished in 1311. FOL. 68V

[15] *The Adoration of the Magi.* (c) Within the initial a groom holds the horses of the Three Kings. In the lower margin Herod orders the massacre of the Innocents. FOL. 69

[16] *The Deposition.* (m) The caryatids, in unusual positions, bear the weight of the frame of the picture. FOL. 75V

[17] *The Presentation in the Temple.* (m) In the margin a monkey performs to the beat of a frame drum. FOL. 76

★

[18] *The Entombment.* (c) As in the Crucifixion, the composition here resembles that used by Duccio in his Maestà. FOL. 82V

[19] *The Flight into Egypt.* (c) The marginal scenes illustrate an apocryphal account which tells how heathen idols fell from their pedestals as Jesus passed by, and the new-sown wheat of a farmer sprang into full bloom. FOL. 83

★

[20] *The Resurrection.* (m) The word "Corr" beneath one of the sleeping soldiers indicates that the text had been corrected through this page. FOL. 94V

[21] *Text Page of Compline.* (m) The original leaf which was opposite the Resurrection is missing. It would have shown the Coronation of the Virgin, the last of the customary illustrations for the Hours of the Virgin.   FOL. 95

★

[22] *A Miracle of Saint Louis.* (c) A queen is shown praying near the tomb of Saint Louis, on which his statue stands. The figures seated by the tomb represent men miraculously healed of blindness by Saint Louis.   FOL. 102V

[23] *The Education of Saint Louis.* (c) Saint Louis, who was crowned king as Louis IX of France when he was twelve, is shown submitting to chastisement by his tutor and father confessor.   FOL. 103

★

[24] *Saint Louis Feeds a Leprous Monk.* (m) Below the miniature a woman and two old men fight with sticks and baskets.   FOL. 123V

[23]

[25] *Text Page of the Office of Saint Louis.* (m) The line endings and the initial are ornamented with monsters. FOL. 124

★

[26] *Saint Louis Administers to the Sick.* (c) The miniature depicts a medieval hospital. Two beggars support the columns. FOL. 142V

[27] *Text Page of the Office of Saint Louis.* (c) The half-monster figures within the initial and in the margins represent a soldier, a musician with a bagpipe, another musician with a trumpet, and a doctor with a flask and his patient. FOL. 143

★

[28] *Saint Louis Washes the Feet of the Poor.* (m) Behind Louis stands his biographer, Joinville, who refused to participate in any such act of humility. FOL. 148V

[29] *Text Page of the Office of Saint Louis.* (m) The half-monk within the initial uses a bellows for a lute. In the upper right a monster-woman looks into a mirror. Below, at the left, a beggar hobbles toward Saint Louis. FOL. 149

[30] *The Miracle of the Breviary.* (c) While Saint Louis was a prisoner of the Saracens during his first crusade, his prayer book, lost during the battle, was miraculously returned to him. FOL. 154V

[31] *Text Page of the Office of Saint Louis.* (c) The grotesque figures within the initial and in the borders include a half-monk with open prayer book, a bagpipe player, and a long-haired grotesque.

FOL. 155

★

[32] *Text Page of the Office of Saint Louis.* (m) The uppermost figure is posing as a fiddle player with a spoon for a bow. Within the initial a monk shows his book to the reader. FOL. 158V

[33] *Text Page of the Office of Saint Louis.* (m) The drolleries represent a soldier with a scimitar and a fist shield, and a figure blowing a shawm. FOL. 159

★

[34] *Saint Louis Burying the Bones of the Crusaders.* (c) In 1253 the Saracens sacked the city of Sidon, killing more than two thousand Christians. When the city was recaptured by the crusaders Saint Louis helped to bury the dead. FOL. 159V

[35] *Text Page of the Office of Saint Louis.* (c) The figures within the initial and in the borders represent humans battling monsters and a monk holding up a chalice. FOL. 160

*

[36] *Text Page of the Office of Saint Louis.* (m) FOL. 164V

[37] *Text Page of the Office of Saint Louis.* (m) Within the initial a rabbit is eating a cabbage-like leaf. The figure in the lower margin flees from a beast which has seized his smock. FOL. 165

*

[38] *The Death of Saint Louis.* (c) Saint Louis died August 25, 1270 near the city of Carthage on his second crusade. He is shown on his deathbed as his soul is carried up to heaven. FOL. 165V

[39] *Text Page of the Office of Saint Louis.* (c) Several of the cavorting figures are playing musical instruments, among which are a triangle with jingles, a mandola, and a harp. FOL. 166

[40] *Text Page of the Office of Saint Louis.* (m) The
first line ends in a mitred bishop with his crozier.
Below is a dog exhausted from chasing the rabbit
running happily away four lines farther down the
page.   FOL. 167V

[41] *Text Page of the Office of Saint Louis.* (m) The
upper marginal figure ties a hank of wool to a spit
which is turned below. The third figure looks ap-
prehensively at the bishop on the opposite page.
Below him are a monster and a rabbit.   FOL. 168

*

[42] *The Procession at Saint-Denis.* (c) On August
25, 1298 Louis IX of France was beatified and his
body was elevated at Saint-Denis, the royal abbey
church near Paris. King Philippe IV, le Bell, and
attendants are shown carrying the relics in pro-
cession.   FOL. 173V

[43] *Text Page of the Office of Saint Louis.* (c) At
the left a monkey climbs an upright marginal decoration. At the right a juggler balances a plate on
a stick to the tunes of several musicians with harp,
bagpipe, and transverse flute.   FOL. 174

[44] *Text Page of the Office of Saint Louis.* (m) The figure in the peaked cap is gesticulating with his fingers, and the monster in the initial chews on his robe.   FOL. 176v

[45] *Text Page of the Office of Saint Louis.* (m) In the margin is the half figure of a hunter about to place a wicker trap, used in bird hunting, over a rabbit. At the same moment he points his spear at a unicorn below.   FOL. 177

★

[46] *Christ Enthroned.* (c) The Saviour, in an attitude of blessing, holds the Gospels and a cross and is surrounded by the symbols of the four Evangelists.   FOL. 182v

[47] *Text Page of the Psalms of Penitence.* (c) Within the initial a monster-woman is playing the cymbals. In the right margin a boy whips a top.
                                       FOL. 183

★

[48] *The Closing Page of the Manuscript.* (m) The initial D is filled by a monster and the final Amen is set off by a rabbit and a grotesque.   FOL. 209v

THE HOURS OF
JEANNE
D'ÉVREUX

ix	b	s philippe s iaque
	c	kl	saint athanase
xix	d	kl	saint croix
viii	e	kl	saint quintace
	f	kl	sainct florentin
xvi	g	kl	saint iehan
v	A		saint nicam
	b	id	saint kach
xiii	c	id	saint ladislas
ij	d	id	saint gordian
	e	id	saint mamert
x	f	id	saint pancrace
	g	id	sainct silluen
xviij	A	id	saint bonifac
vii	b	id	saint ysidoru

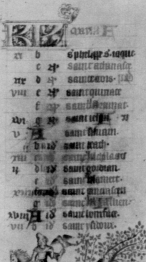

Incipiunt scipie le marie iur
gls scdm usum pdicator.

seculorum. Amen.

Uenite adoremus.

Regem uirginis filium de
mite adoremus. Hymnus

Quem terra pontus
ecthera colunt ado
rant predicant trinam
regentem machinam
claustrum marie baiu
lat.

Qui luna sol et omnia

deseruunt p tempora
perfusa celi gratia gestat
puelle uiscera.

Beata mater munere
cuius supnus artifer
mundiem pugillo con
tinens uentris sub arcta
clausus est.

Beata celi nuntio faci
dit sancto spiritu desi de
ratus gentibz cuius per

eus adlaudes
madiutonium

eus ad iu̇.
madiurorūi

in nomine domini: qui
fecit celum et terram

Gloria patri et filio et
spiritui sancto.

Sicut erat. ps dd

Qui confidunt in
domino sicut mon
tyon non commouebit
in eternum qui habitat

in ierlm

Montes in circuitu eius

et dominus manduta
populi sui: et hec nunc
usqz in seculum.
Quia non relinquet
dominus virgam pecca
torum sup sortem iusto
rum ut non extendant
iusti ad iniquitatem
manus suas.
Bene fac domine bo
nis et rectis corde.

eus ad sextam.
m adintorium

eus ad nonam
ma diutorium

eus ad vͥs
madiutoziũ

Con.

uo tum uouit deo iacob.

Si introiero in tabernac
ulum domus mee si as
cendero in lectum strati
mei.

Si dedero sompnium o
culis meis. ⁊ palpebris me
is dormitationem.

Et requiem temporib;
meis donec inueniam locu
dño tabernacula dm deo iacob

Anapuit hoze bn ludoui
a fcdm usu predicatoz

omine labia me
a aperies

eiiſ maduito
iuini meum

tende.

Domine ad adiuuand
me festina

Gloria patri et filio et
spiritui sancto

Sicut erat in principio
et nunc et semper et in se
cula seculorum. amen.
alleluia. *R̃*. Sunt. *ps*

Dominus reg̃. d̃
naut de coꝛei in

Ad p̄mam
eus m ad
iutorium
meum in
tende. Domine ad adiuuan
dum me festina. Gloria patri et filio
spiritui sancto. Sicut erat in principi
o et nunc et semper et in

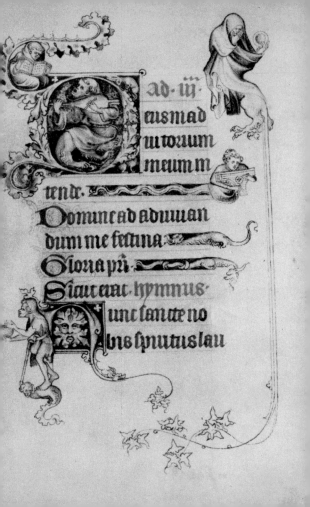

ad· iij·
eius m ad
uitorium
meum in

tende·

Domine ad adiuuan
dum me festina·

Gloria pri·

Sicut erat· hymnus·

Nunc santte no

bis spiritus lau

Ad sextam.
eus in ad
iutorium
meum in
tende.

Domine ad adiuuan
dum me festina.
Gloria patri filio et
spiritui sancto.
Sicut erat in principi
o et nunc et semper in secu

Et elegit eum ex omni
carne. ✠✠✠✠✠
Domine exaudi ora-
nem meam.
Et clamor meus ad
te veniat.
Oremus. oratio
Innue nobis do-
mine quæsumus sicut
beatus ludouicus confes-
sor tuus meruit tibi di-

gne famulari meruit:
ita nos facias eius a
pud te precibus adiuuari.
p dominum nostrum
ihesum xpistum filiu
tuum. Qui tecum uiuit
et regnat deus p omni
a secula seculorum.

Amen.

Bndicamus domino.

Deo gracias.

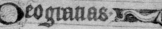

ad ix

eus in ad
iutorium
meum in

tende.

Domine ad adiuua
dium me festina.

Gloria patri et filio
spiritui sancto.

Sicut erat in prin
pio et nunc et semper

giā qualem nullus
habuit ante eum rex
Deo gratias · R̄ m̄
In fide et lenitate ipsius
sanctum fecit illum. v̄
Et elegit eum ex omni
carne. sanctum fecit
Gloria patri et filio et
spūi sčo · In fide et le. v̄
Iustum non dereliquit
dominus · s3 a pčōnibz liā

rauit eum. Oremus.

Beata ludouica oro
confeſſoris tui
queſumus domine p
ces nobis glorioſe ſub
ueniant quem deuca
terreni regimuris ad ce
leſtis regni auriam per
ducat. p dominum.

Benedicamus domino
Deo gratias.

lou

Ad vesperas.
eus in ad
iutorium
meum in

tende.

Domine ad adiuuan

dum me festina.

Gloria patri et filio

spiritu sancto.

Sicut erat in principi

o et nunc et semper et in

u suo.

Hec est generatio que
rentium eum querenti
um faciem dei iacob

Attollite portas prin
cipes uestras: et eleuami
ni porte eternales et in
troibit rex glorie.

Quis est iste rex glorie.
dominus fortis et potens.
dominus potens in pre

uo.

Attollite portas prin
cipes uras et eleuamini
porte eternales et introi
bit rex glorie.

Quis est iste rex glori
e. dominus uirtutum ipse
est rex glorie.

Gloria patri et filio z
spiritui sancto ex

Sicut erat. ani.

con̄.

Ad comple

onuerten̄
deus salu
taris n̄r.

Et auerte iram tuam
a nobis.

Deus in adiutori
um meum inte
de.

Domine ad adiuuan
dum me festina.

Gloria patri et filio
spiritui sancto.
Sicut erat in principi
o et nunc et semper et in se
cula seculorum.
Amen. Antiphona
Iustificauit dominus san
ctam regem suum coram illis
nice terminus in regno
suorum. Capitulum
Consummatus

in breui explcuit mul
ta tempora placata e
nim erat deo anima il
lius

Deo gratias. k. uim

In manus tuas spiritum
deus commendauit. v

Rer suum iudens exitum.
deus commendauit.

Gloria patri et filio et spiritu
sancto. In manus ymn

Incipiunt septem psal
mi peniten
tiales.
Domine
ne in furo
re tuo arguas me neq̃
mira tua corripias me.
Miserere mei domine
quoniam infirmus sū
sana me domine quoni
am conturbata sunt os

Deus cui proprium
est miserei sem
p̃ et parce suscipe deprecā
tionem nram et quos de
lictorum caena con
stringit miseratio tue pi
etas absoluat· per x̃m
dominum nrm
amen·